A Big City A B C

ALLAN MOAK

Tundra Books

Original edition published by Tundra Books, Montreal, 1984
This edition published by Tundra Books, Toronto, 2002

Copyright © 1984, 2002 by Allan Moak

Published in Canada by Tundra Books,
481 University Avenue, Toronto, Ontario M5G 2E9

Published in the United States by Tundra Books of Northern New York,
P.O. Box 1030, Plattsburgh, New York 12901

Library of Congress Catalog Number: 2001095520

National Library of Canada Cataloguing in Publication Data

Moak, Allan
    A big city ABC

ISBN 0-88776-587-4

1. English language – Alphabet – Juvenile literature. 2. Toronto (Ont.)
 – Pictorial works – Juvenile literature. I. Title

PE1155.M62 2002   j421'.1   C2001-903220-X

We acknowledge the support of the Canada Council for the Arts and the
Ontario Arts Council for our publishing program.

We acknowledge the financial support of the Government of Canada through
the Book Publishing Industry Development Program for our publishing activities.

Design: Cindy Reichle

Printed in Hong Kong, China

1 2 3 4 5 6   07 06 05 04 03 02

 A is for Art a

B is for Baseball

 C is for Castle

D is for Deli

E is for Excavation

F is for Fireworks

 G is for Greenhouse

 H is for Horses

I is for Island Ferry

 J is for Junk Store

K is for Kites

L is for Lifeguard

M is for Market

 N is for Neighborhood

O

O is for October

🌰

 P is for Park

Q   Q is for Queen   q

R is for Rink

S is for Science Centre

 T is for Tugboat

 U is for Umbrella

V is for Variety Store

 W is for Winter

 X is for the EX

 Y is for Yuletide

Z is for Zoo

TORONTO

Toronto, Canada's largest city and one of the great cities of the world, means different things to different people. For some, it is the business center of the country, with its soaring office towers and banks. For others, it is the arts capital, with its galleries, theaters, radio and television studios.

My Toronto is for children; I see it through children's eyes.
Many of the things that children like most in this great city, I like too.

A – Art: The Art Gallery of Ontario was opened in 1900 – more than a hundred years ago. For years it was named the Art Gallery of Toronto. Its exhibitions of Canadian and foreign art have attracted thousands of people, young and old. The world's largest collection of abstract sculptures by the English sculptor Henry Moore is in this gallery. Outside, for all to see, is a special Henry Moore work loved by children, who can climb on it to their heart's content.

B – Baseball: The Blue Jays is the major baseball team in Toronto. The team mascots are two fast-moving people named Ace and Diamond. They perform back flips for the fans at the Skydome in downtown Toronto. The Skydome is said to be the world's largest multipurpose retractable domed stadium. This means that thousands of Blue Jay fans can watch baseball when the great roof is open to the skies in fine weather, and when the roof is closed in cold and wet weather. The Skydome was first opened in June 1989.

C – Castle: Casa Loma stands on a hill overlooking midtown Toronto. Sir Henry Mill Pellatt's 98-room medieval-style castle was completed in 1914, and its large towers and secret passageways have made it a fairy-tale place for children ever since. After a snowfall, the castle looks even more beautiful.

D – Deli: Next to painting, I think eating is the most fun. Toronto has some of the finest delis anywhere, and I love to explore them. The smells that greet me – spicy sausages, sweet pastries, pickles, cheeses, even bird's nest soup – seem to bring the world into one small place.

E – Excavation: It is no use telling you where I painted this huge hole in the earth in downtown Toronto because by the time you read this, it won't be there. In the many years I have lived in Toronto, the city has been rebuilt before my very eyes. Can *you* walk by a construction site without stopping to watch? Do the cranes remind you of toys in a sandbox?

F – Fireworks: Traditionally fireworks, invented centuries ago in China, spray the night skies with color and beauty. They are set off to mark special occasions – Canada Day, Victoria Day, and the Canadian National Exhibition (CNE), which attracts thousands of girls and boys and their parents to one of the greatest displays in Canada. The Princes' Gates at the CNE were officially opened in 1927 by the Prince of Wales, later King Edward VIII, and his younger brother, the Duke of York, who became King George V.

G – Greenhouse: Allan Gardens at Sherbourne and Carlton Streets was developed in 1909 in the Victorian style. It is a tropical paradise of plants and flowers. Particularly in winter, when the city's outdoor gardens are asleep, Allan Gardens is a wonderful place to visit. The greenhouse and park around it cover a whole city block.

H – Horses: While Metropolitan Toronto's great police force patrols the streets of the city in cars, on bicycles, and on foot, they also have a stable of expertly trained horses ridden by similarly expertly trained police officers. These officers roam the city streets, particularly in summer, mostly in pairs. When there are great crowds of people, they often assist those police officers who are on foot.

I – Island Ferry: The ferryboat *Sam McBride* was named after a Toronto mayor who first took office in 1928. It crosses the harbor to the Toronto Islands: Ward's, Hanlan's, and Centre Island, where families can go for picnics. Centre Island is a fine spot for watching birds and people.

J – Junk Store: I love to collect junk, so painting this shop on Queen Street West was great fun for me. Old toys, old machinery, old anything – if I keep any of it long enough, it might be called antique. Toronto is one of the few big cities to still have streetcars, so I put one in the background. Have you ever ridden on a bright red streetcar?

K – Kites: Every summer in Toronto, kites fly in our parks and open spaces. The old lighthouse in this painting was moved from its original site to Lakeshore Boulevard, near the Princes' Gates of the CNE. Here, on the harbor front where the breezes are light and airy, seagulls join the kites in the clear blue sky.

L – Lifeguard: A summer's day at the beach wouldn't be complete without a swim and ice cream. The Eastern Beaches Park covers the waterfront from Ashbridges Bay to the eastern city lights. Here, I painted Kew Beach, with its boardwalk and bicycle path. The lifeguard keeps a lookout for emergencies in the water.

M – Market: Children don't always like shopping for food, but Kensington Market, near College Street and Spadina Avenue, offers so much to see, hear, and smell that a visit there is like a little trip around the world. It used to be known as the Jewish market, but today nearly every immigrant group is well represented.

N – Neighborhood: The narrow back laneways of west Toronto are wonderful play areas for children. Hockey is often practiced in them all year round. This painting was inspired by the lane behind a house I used to live in on Palmerston Boulevard.

O – October: I wanted to include an autumn scene in this book. The fun of playing in the leaves is a special Toronto treat. We are lucky to have so many trees that our city has actually been called the City of Trees. The house in the painting is where I once lived on Westmoreland Avenue.

P – Park: Toronto has hundreds of parks and "parkettes." On a summer's day, the wading pools are asplash with children keeping cool, and the ice-cream trucks with their jingling bells are never far away. This park is near Palmerston Boulevard and Ulster Street.

Q – Queen: Toronto is often called the Queen City, and reminders of Queen Victoria are everywhere. Her monument stands in front of the legislative buildings in Queen's Park, where the provincial Parliament of Ontario meets. The brownstone and granite buildings were designed by architect R. A. Waite, and opened in 1963.

R – Rink: How many other cities can boast a skating rink for children and parents right in front of city hall? And what a place to skate! Situated in Nathan Phillips Square, it is a lasting monument to one of Toronto's most innovative mayors. The sculpture called *The Archer* that you see here is by famous English sculptor Henry Moore.

S – Science Centre: The Ontario Science Centre at Don Mills Road and Eglinton Avenue East is a busy and exciting place to visit. Children can play astronaut on a simulated spaceflight, try papermaking, or take part in a static electricity demonstration. I have shown part of Rowland Emett's *Magical Machines* called "The Afternoon Tea-Train to Wisteria Halt."

T – Tugboat: The old steam-powered tugboat the *Ned Hanlan*, named in honor of a famous Toronto athlete, served for many years in the Toronto harbor. It was retired, restored, and placed on permanent display at the CNE grounds next to the Marine Museum.

U – Umbrella: When it rains in Toronto, the umbrellas that go up make colorful patterns on the streets. I chose Parliament Street as the background because its architecture recalls Toronto's earlier years. The spire of St. James Cathedral towers above the roofs.

V – Variety Store: Every neighborhood has its favorite variety store, as popular with children as with their moms and dads. This one is on Dovercourt Road, at the corner of Shanly Street. Have you a favorite?

W – Winter: When Toronto gets a big snowfall, children love to throw snowballs and build snow forts. In this laneway in west Toronto, children are also busy building snowmen and creating snow angels.

X – The EX: Even though it doesn't start with the letter X, it sounds like it does. The EX, or CNE, is held the last three weeks of August, ending on Labor Day. It has an exciting midway and exhibits from around the world. Older Torontonians remember the EX as one of the happiest places of their childhood, and children today await it like Christmas. Exhibition Park is on the shores of Lake Ontario.

Y – Yuletide: Around Christmastime each year, Toronto lights up as we decorate our homes to welcome the holiday season. The houses in this painting are on Mutual Street, in the downtown area. Sometimes we are lucky and have a white Christmas.

Z – Zoo: The Metro Toronto Zoo, on Meadowvale Road north of Highway 401, is one of the largest in the world. It was just too large for one painting, so I composed a fanciful zoo showing children painting the animals, and placed it in the harbor area, with Ontario Place and the CN Tower in the background.

And now, paint A BIG CITY ABC of your own favorite places!

Allan Moak